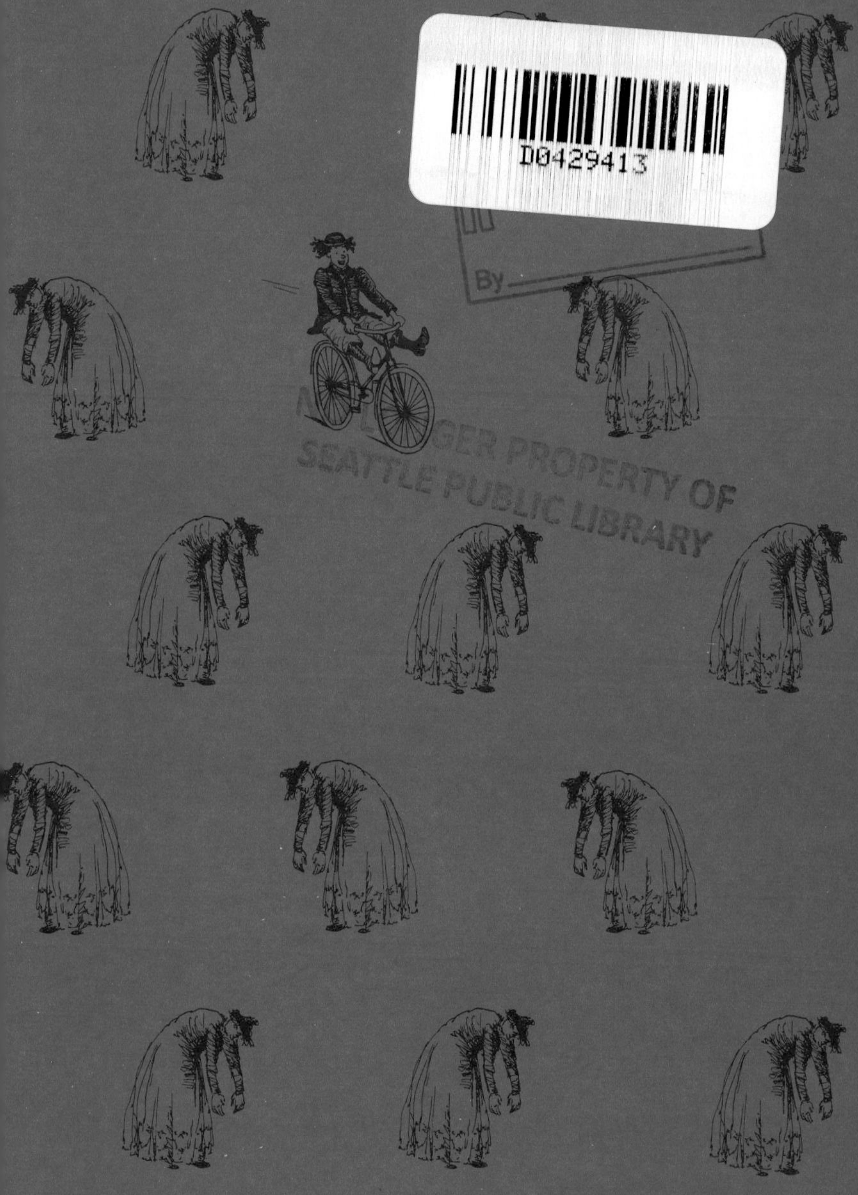

THE TROUBLE WITH WOMEN

THE
TROUBLE
WITH
WOMEN

JACKY FLEMING

Andrews McMeel
Publishing®

a division of Andrews McMeel Universal

" TAKE NOBODY'S WORD FOR IT "

motto of the Royal Society

In the Olden Days there were no women which is why you don't come across them in history lessons at school. There were men and quite a few of them were Geniuses.

Then there were a few women but their heads were very small so they were rubbish at everything apart from needlework and croquet.

Women were occasionally allowed to study but not to get a degree in anything because of their small heads.

Very occasionally a woman would learn a foreign language, go abroad to study, and come back qualified as a doctor, but that didn't prove anything except that women cause trouble as soon as you allow them out.

Women weren't allowed out at night because of their poor night vision. They were also too emotional to take anywhere so mostly they stayed in and wept, sometimes hysterically.

As Darwin said by keeping women at home their achievements were paltry compared to men's, which proved women were biologically inferior. And he should know because he was a Genius.

You probably learned about him 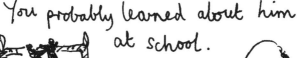 at school.

For a long time there were no black women. Everyone was white, except for Sarah Forbes Bonetta who was brought up by Queen Victoria. She was very clever for a girl, as well as headstrong and opinionated, so she was married off before she set a bad example.

So you won't find HER in history your lessons.

Queen Victoria was herself a rare example of Early Woman, shown here holding something unaided.

But not for long.

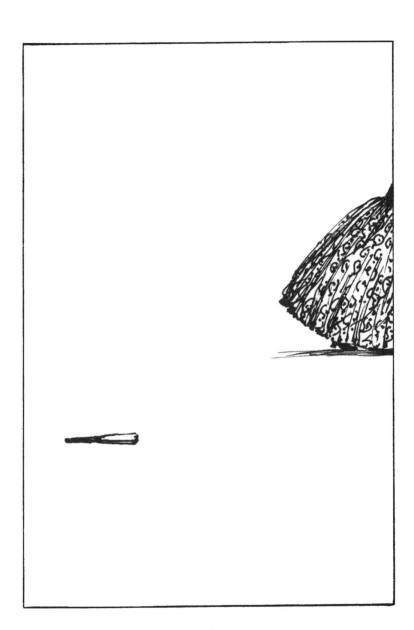

The first woman lived in a Domestic Sphere.

Inside the Sphere women did things which weren't too demanding like childcare, scrubbing the floor, washing the sheets and curtains, sewing on buttons, and coal mining.

Women with domestic servants could devote themselves to their embroidery samplers,

which speak to us
across the centuries.

Women who ventured outside the Domestic Sphere were known as Fallen Women. There were 6,722 Fallen Women.

There were many ways of becoming Fallen, including having a side part, having your own mind, speaking out loud instead of just thinking it, and not remaining a virgin after giving birth.

Only women could Fall.

Jean-Jacques Rousseau, Restless Genius of the Enlightenment and keen flasher, said girls needed to be thwarted from an early age so that their natural role in pleasing men would come more naturally to them. He put his own children in an orphanage to be thwarted.

RESTLESS GENIUS

Some women who had not been sufficiently thwarted escaped the Domestic Sphere on horseback, camel, and bicycle. They had to sit sidesaddle to avoid a Sexual Awakening.

...which would ruin their Prospects.

Women were more concerned about their skirts getting caught up in the wheels, and sat astride wearing Bloomers which turned them into lesbians.

Bloomers were made illegal in Chattanooga.

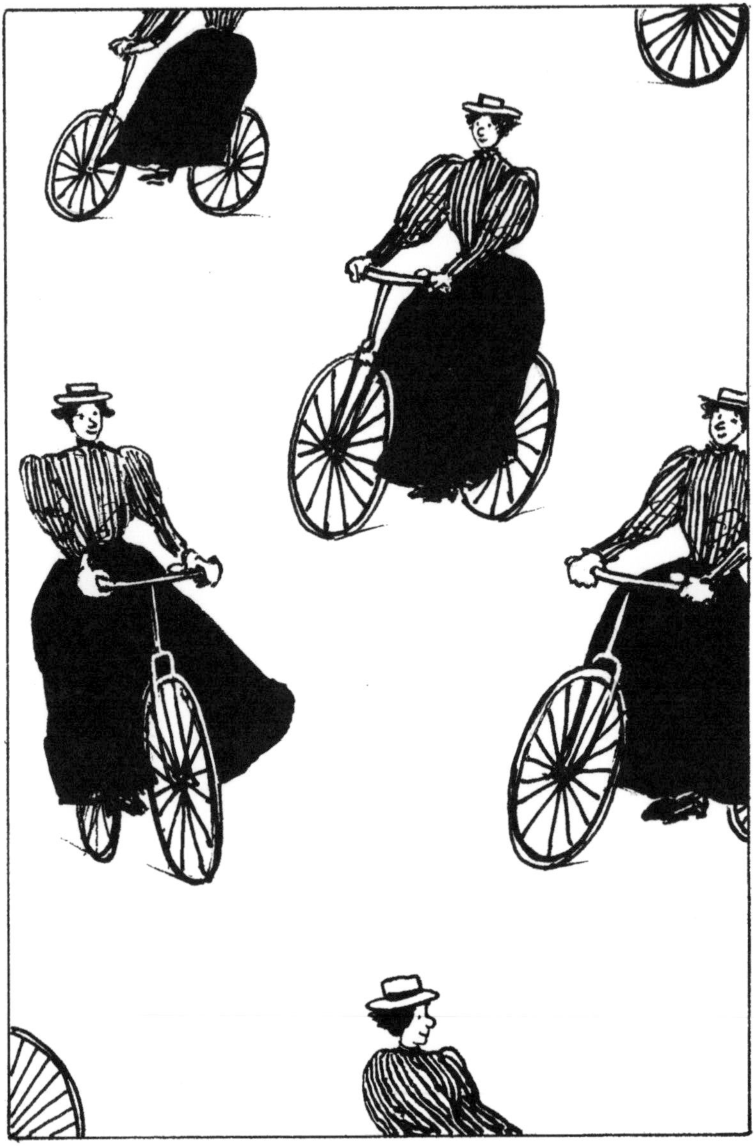

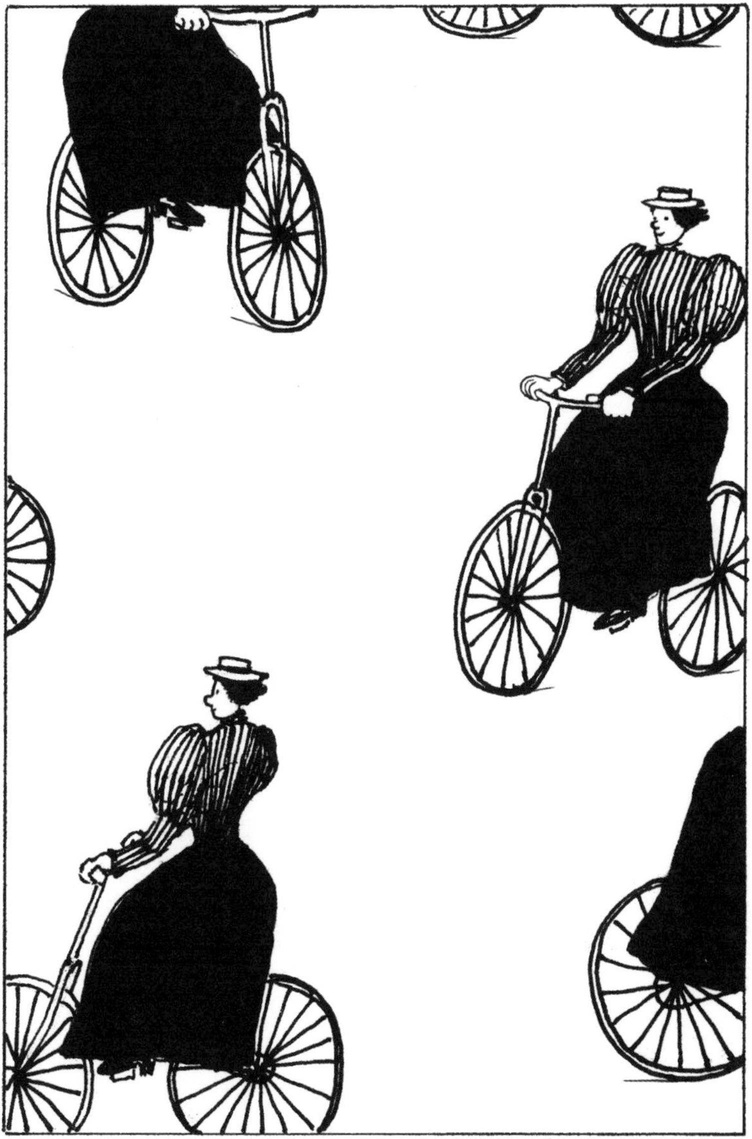

Big frocks were an early form of handbag. Women could carry on their person sewing accessories, cosmetics, and essentials for childbirth.

The frocks may have made sporting activity more cumbersome, but women's skeletons weren't designed for sports in the first place.

There were other reasons why women were not suited to sport. Women could not run fast and were prone to overheat.

Unsightly muscles could do serious harm to women's marriage prospects.

There was also the ever-present risk of sporting accidents which could result in a permanent loss of virginity.

Swimming didn't come naturally to women either, and many drowned despite the heavy flannel bathing costumes, which protected their virtue at the same time as preventing them from catching a chill.

A more risqué but modern swimsuit was the sack with holes worn with swimming boots.

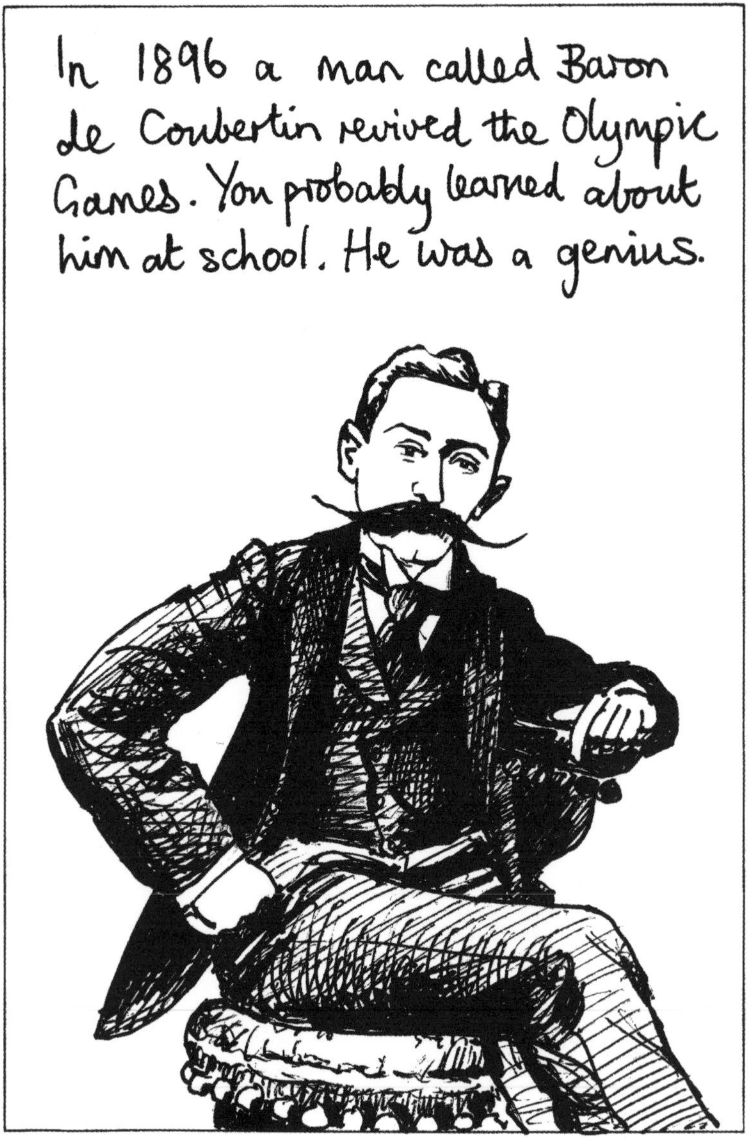
In 1896 a man called Baron de Coubertin revived the Olympic Games. You probably learned about him at school. He was a genius.

He said it would be an abject
sight watching women trying to
throw a ball, but that they
looked more natural clapping.

By the 5th Olympic Games there were just enough women to form a swimming team with 1 extra as a chaperone.

Notice the chaperone has already damaged her marriage prospects.

It wasn't until the 1960s that women were allowed to uncross their arms, and even then only in emergencies.

Meanwhile in America, Annie Oakley could shoot the ash off her husband's cigarette, but it wasn't an Olympic event.

At least she had dainty feet.

Nan Aspinwall rode her horse across America, finishing on the 12th floor of New York's City Hall. But that wasn't an Olympic event either.

35

Early women did not need an education as they were feebleminded. Female brains were not only smaller, but they were made of a soft, spongy, lightweight material.

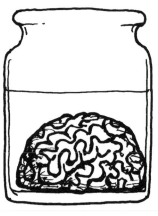

MALE BRAIN

FEMALE BRAIN

Once girls had learned sixty different embroidery stitches there was no more room to learn anything else.

Frontal lobe for original and creative thought

Frontal lobe for neat copying. Empty space where original thought occurs

ACTUAL SIZE

Geniuses like Darwin's cousin were fascinated by why all geniuses were male. It had them baffled.

BAFFLED GENIUS

They made lists of eminent men, which proved that female intellect was puny, but in a good way.

Girls who weren't servants, slaves, or coal miners were too fragile for schooling, but they could always eavesdrop if they had brothers.

Eavesdropping was hampered by hairdos which covered up the ears.

In the 700 years between Hildegard of Bingen and Jane Austen, women writing was frowned upon because it required Thought, which interfered with childbirth.

Women found lifting a pen very tiring as it caused chlorosis which disrupted blood flow and in some cases led to uterine prolapse.

Or was that the corsets?

Even if corsets did prevent breathing, women collapsed without them, so not wearing one wasn't an option.

And corsets made women look
prettier in an ill sort of way
even if their internal organs
were a bit squashed up...

whereas riding a bicycle
gave women men's legs
and looked unsightly.

Having men's legs could cause immense shock on the wedding night, and prevent a marriage from being consummated.

Studying also had unattractive side effects, notably hair loss. Notice that in this early portrait of Anna Maria van Schurman she has a full head of hair.

In this later portrait, after studying Latin, Greek, Hebrew, French, English, Italian, Spanish, Aramaic, Turkish, Arabic, Samaritan, Persian, Ethiopic, Syriac, glass engraving, and portraiture, she has noticeably less hair.

When she attended lectures she had to sit behind a curtain, obviously, as eavesdropping was allowed but not actual studying.

When African slave Phillis Wheatley wrote poetry, 18 men came to assess whether that was possible.

In the end it was simpler just to disguise yourself as a man.

As Ruskin said, "woman's intellect is not for invention or creation.... Her great function is praise."

Genius
well done
so clever
marvelous

Ruskin's genius was to open people's eyes to the beauty of nature, except for his wife's body which he found disgusting – leading to endless speculation about what horrified him on his wedding night,

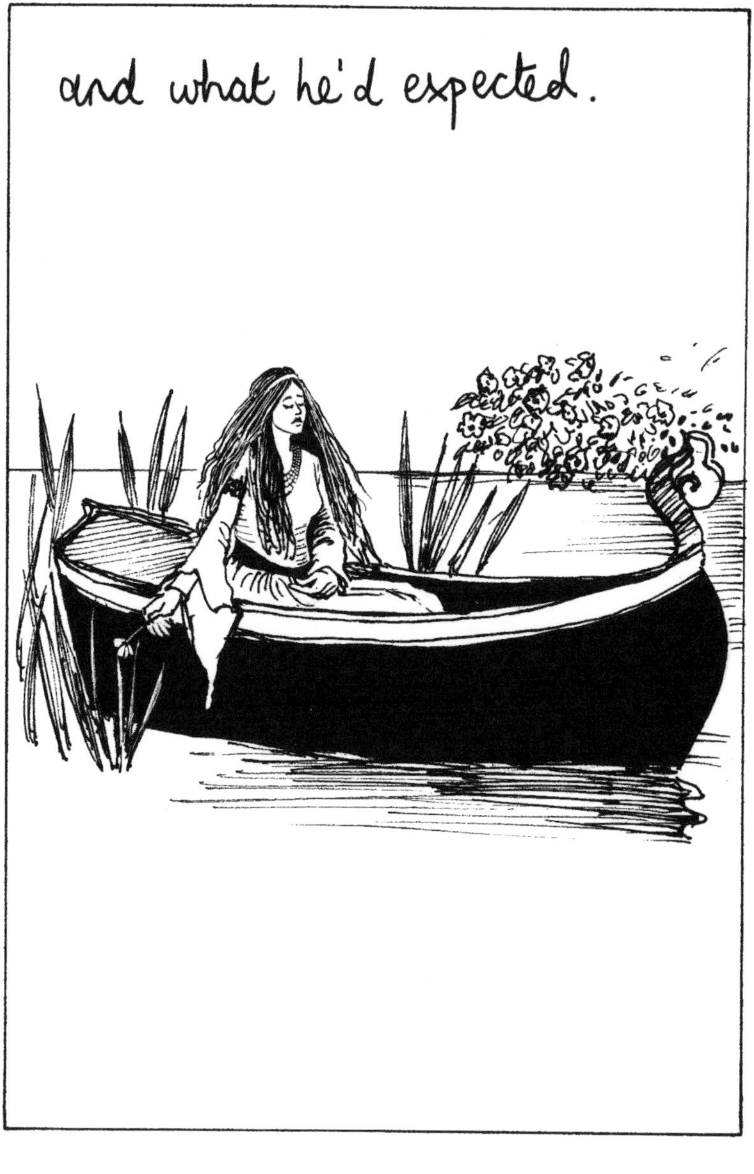
and what he'd expected.

As creativity uses a part of the brain missing in women, most of us can only think of ~~two~~ three women artists, recognizable by the weakness of the feminine hand,

WEAK
HANDS

which can only hold a brush
for a short period of time.

Domestic servants, slaves, and women who worked in coal mines had men's hands, which served as a warning to women who wanted to leave the Domestic Sphere.

MEN'S HANDS

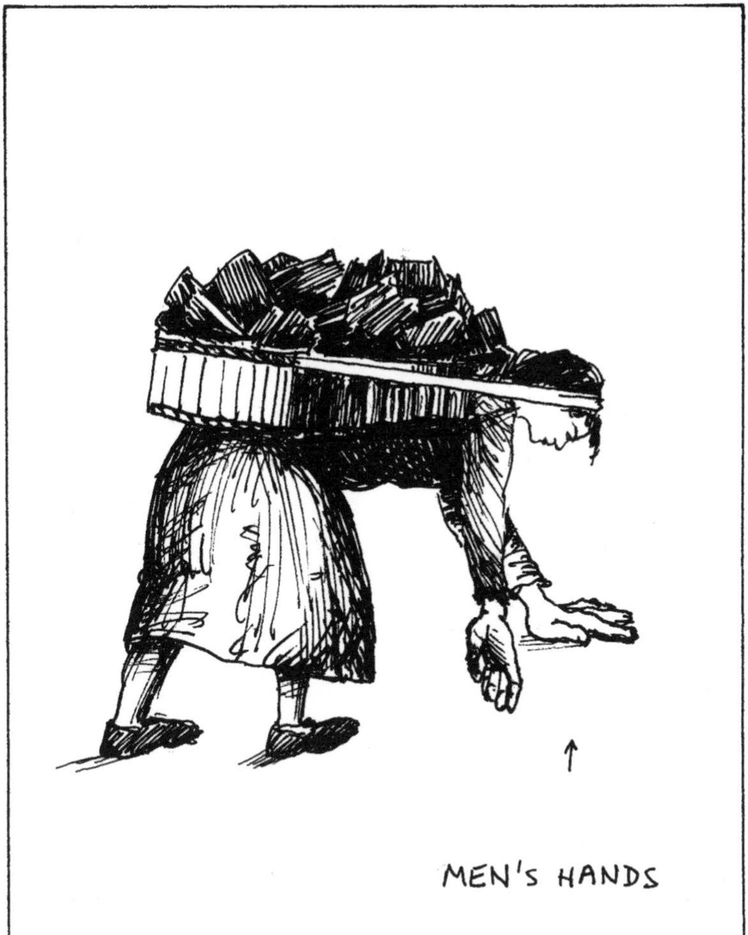
MEN'S HANDS

Even with men's hands women could only make small art, mediocre art, or even big art with horses in it, but never great art, as only men can do that.

MEDIOCRE
ART

Critics were quick to spot
the weakness of the feminine hand
once they knew who the art was by.

Women were excluded from Art Academies, but flower painting with added knickknacks was more ladylike anyway, and you could do it in the Domestic Sphere.

Some women, like Marianne North, willfully misunderstood and went off painting flowers all over the world without a chaperone.

Some art by women has accidentally been considered great, a mistake easily rectified by placing it in the Dustbin of History.

DUSTBIN OF HISTORY

Women have been retrieving
each other from the Dustbin of History
for several thousand years now...

but have been unable to produce a Female Picasso, which must come as something of a relief given the suicide rate of his muses.

Picasso said women were made for suffering, which makes a change from needlework or clapping.

As well as languishing in the Dustbin of History, you can spot women artists as wives or girlfriends in the background of documentaries about great men.

Great philosopher Schopenhauer said women had proved incapable of any truly great or original achievement in art, or in anything at all, because they lacked genius hair.

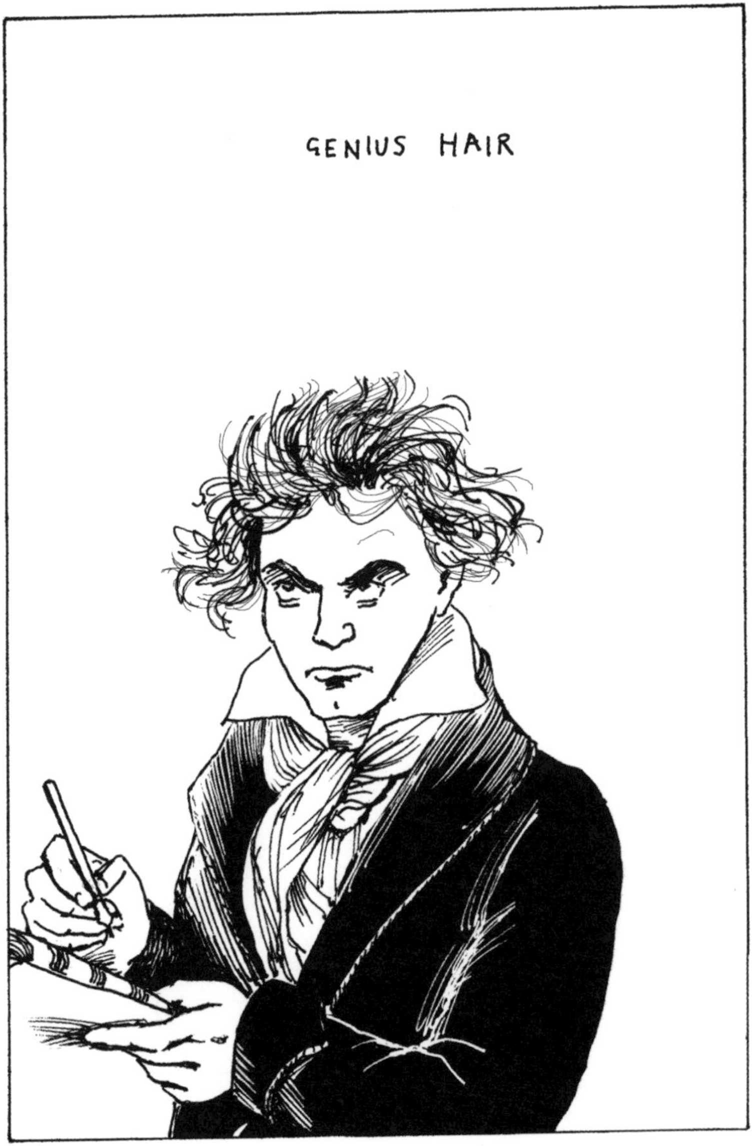
GENIUS HAIR

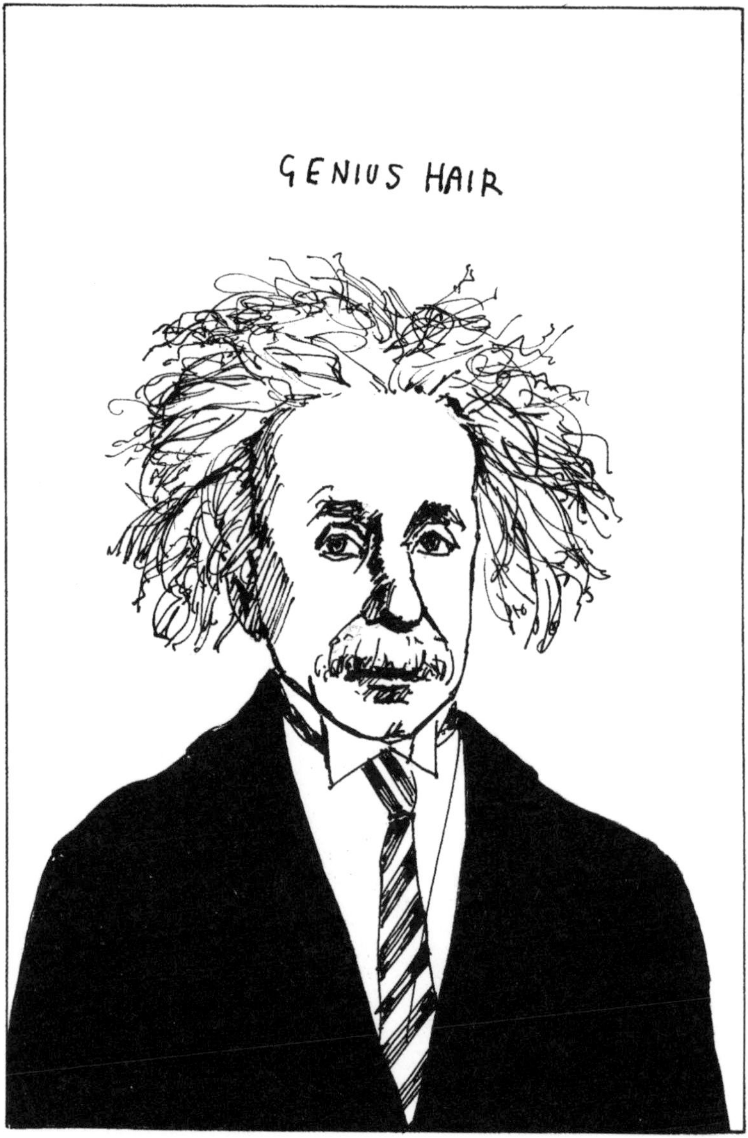
GENIUS HAIR

Darwin's friend and colleague George Romanes said although women were the losers intellectually, having five ounces less brain, they were better at soft furnishings and disappointment.

Which was fortunate.

Due to natural selection and the sexual preference for girls with less intelligence, genius hair in women has largely died out.

Women with genius hair risked being put in asylums, as it was seen as a sign of mental instability.

Sexual selection favored women with hair like a horse.

Marie Curie is the only female scientist since women began. Girls weren't allowed to study science because their reproductive organs made them irrational, and abstract thought doesn't get the curtains hung. They were allowed to collect insects as you can do that in your own garden.

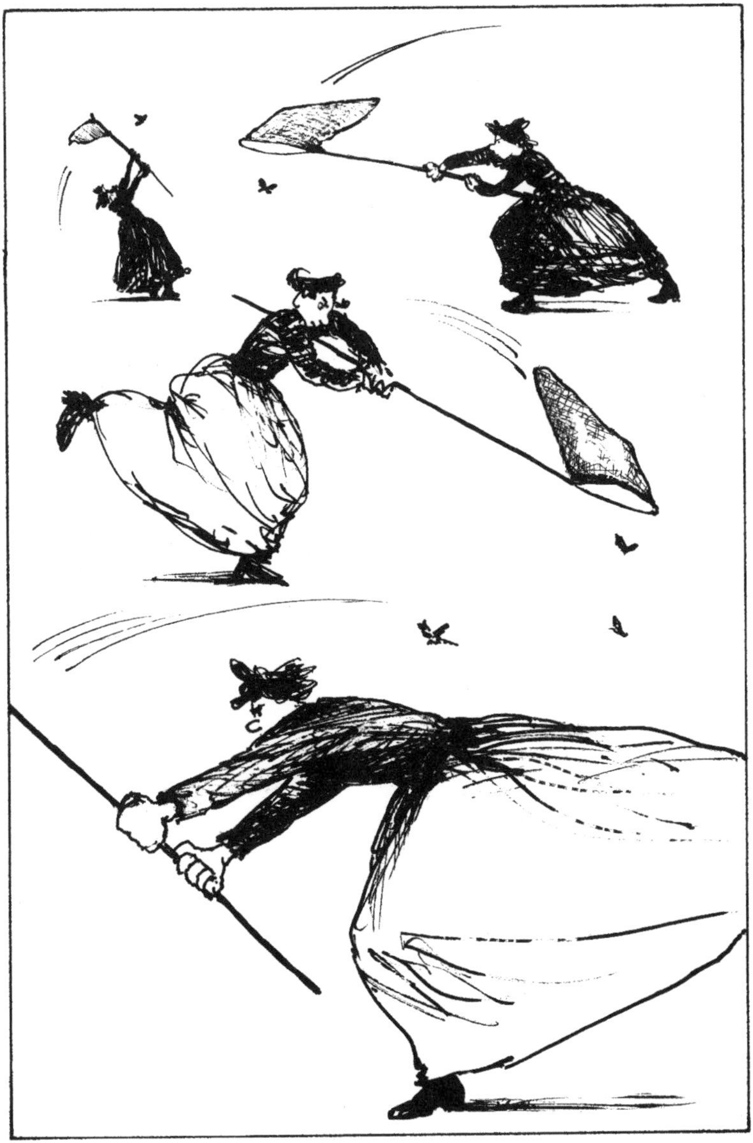

Girls were too emotional to be objective, but they could arrange their insect collections in a pretty way.

TOO EMOTIONAL

Mary Ball's collection was so extensive male scientists came to see it, and noted the accuracy of her observations, so rare in a woman.

Dr. Edward Clarke, a Harvard professor, said it was possible for a girl to study hard and do well in everything, but it would damage her health for the rest of her life, and her children would be shriveled.

SHRIVELED
CHILD

Women who studied science also ran the risk of growing a beard. As Immanuel Kant pointed out, if a woman grew a beard it would "weaken the charms with which she exercises her great power over the other sex."

The Marquise du Châtelet put herself at serious risk of growing a beard and ruining her reproductive system by dividing 9 figures by 9 other figures entirely in her head.

$$532739845 \overline{)924168328}$$

Darwin suggested male beards could be due to natural selection, but he made no mention of baldness and how that happened.

NATURALLY SELECTED BEARDS

GRAVITAS BEARD

RATIONAL BEARD

GOD BEARD

AUTHORITY BEARD

EXPERTISE BEARD

GENIUS BEARD

WRITER BEARD

THINKER BEARD

There were other obstacles to women studying science such as the diameter of their big frocks.

Did I mention being too emotional?

On the whole women were not welcome in scientific societies as they looked out of place,

and it sent out the wrong message - that women CAN do science.

As Maupassant, father of the short story pointed out, any attempt by any woman to achieve anything was futile.

He said women have two parts to play, both of them charming — Love and Maternity. Not isolating radium and polonium.

Women were barned from the
Vatican Observatory except during
daylight hours.

It wasn't until clothes were more bendy that women could access equipment.

By moving their belongings around to the back women could reach things unassisted, but between 1881 and 1889 they couldn't sit down.

Schopenhauer said only men had the total objectivity necessary for genius, and that you only had to look at a woman's shape to see that she wasn't intended for too much mental or physical work.

Emmy Noether, mathematician, was this shape.

Einstein described her as the most significant creative mathematical genius... since women began, not since the world began, obviously. She wasn't actually paid or anything.

Her students complained about her appearance, but she was oblivious.

NOETHER'S THEOREM

Her small brain was already full of the beautiful symmetry of the universe.

You see how pretty Emmy Noether was before she damaged her prospects with too much algebra? That's the trouble with women — they always take things too far.

Marie Curie asked for a dark wedding dress she could wear afterward in the laboratory, showing a dismal grasp of women's natural frivolity.

A few hysterical women even wanted to become doctors, when what they clearly needed was treatment for penis envy, but Freud, Genius, hadn't invented it yet.

Freud kept this painting, of Professor Charot demonstrating hysteria at his asylum for women, on his wall.

It shows that doctors are men, female patients are attractive under hypnosis, and Professor Charot looked like Marlon Brando.

Frederic Carpenter Skey gave lectures on hysteria. He said the typical hysteric was a female exhibiting more than usual force of character, bold riders having plenty of what is termed nerve.

He probably just meant a woman who hadn't been thwarted.

BOLD RIDER

The "hysteric" in Freud's painting, Louise Augustine Gleizes, got sick of posing for Charcot's camera, and for the spectacle of his public Tuesday lectures.
She escaped from his asylum dressed as a man, and was never heard of again.

Henry Maudsley warned women that studying medicine would cause withering of the breasts. He was consultant to the Archduchess Carlota Empress of Mexico and favored a gravitas beard. In later life he sported the god beard.

Medical staff and students did what they could to stop women's breasts from withering. They blocked their way into exams, and pelted them with peas and rubbish.

When that didn't work they tried the
old sheep-in-the-exam-hall trick,

... and an inconvenient, early form of trolling, which meant leaving the house and posting anonymous letters, as there was no internet.

INCONVENIENT
TROLLING

These were the first four women who qualified as doctors, but lost their sex appeal. It's a tragedy which could easily have been avoided as there were plenty of doctors already.

DR. OKAMI

DR. LEE CRUMPLER

DR. JOSHI

DR. ISLAMBOOLY

If we were going to be picky they weren't the first. Margaret Bulkley had already chosen the dress-as-a-man option over destitution, and become James Barry, brilliant army surgeon.

How she did it with such a small head remains a mystery.

All her dogs were called Psyche.

PSYCHE   PSYCHE   PSYCHE   PSYCHE

Darwin's assistant Romanes said "We rarely find in women that firm tenacity of purpose and determination to overcome obstacles which is characteristic of what we call a manly mind."

MANLY MIND

"In other words women are usually less able to concentrate their attention; their minds are more prone to what is called 'wandering,' and we seldom find that they have specialized their studies or pursuits to the same extent as is usual among men."

WANDERING MIND

For 14 years former slave Eliza Grier alternated each year of study with a year of cotton-picking, until she'd qualified as a teacher and a doctor — demonstrating exactly the lack of manly purpose Romanes was on about, so you won't learn about HER in school.

WOMANLY
WAVERING MIND

well
done

PRIVATE
INCOME

FIRM
TENACITY OF
PURPOSE

DETERMINATION TO
OVERCOME OBSTACLES

The World Anti-Slavery Convention in 1840 spent the first day debating whether or not to allow in the female delegates, who'd traveled 3,000 miles to be there. They decided not, but allowed them to sit behind a curtain as spectators.

This led to the First Wave of feminism, bringing to an end two thousand years during which women achieved nothing worth mentioning.

There were a lot of waves before the First Wave, but they're in the Dustbin.

Only men had reached the evolutionary level of decision makers, so they had to decide what to make decisions about, then vote on it themselves. In 1875 they raised the age of consent from 12 to 13.

As women keep their baby teeth into adulthood – a characteristic they share with the butterfly – they have been kept out of the Public Sphere, leaving them free to decide which ribbon to buy, or whether to live as a man.

Schopenhauer put it succinctly when he said women remain big children, "a sort of intermediate stage between the child and the man, who is the real human being, 'man.'"

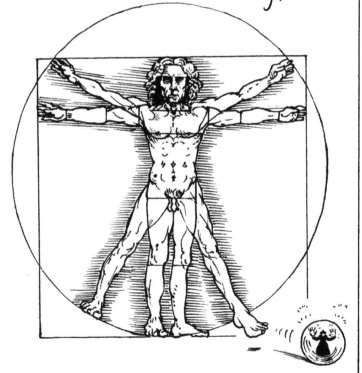

The evolution of women had quite simply stopped before they had finished developing.

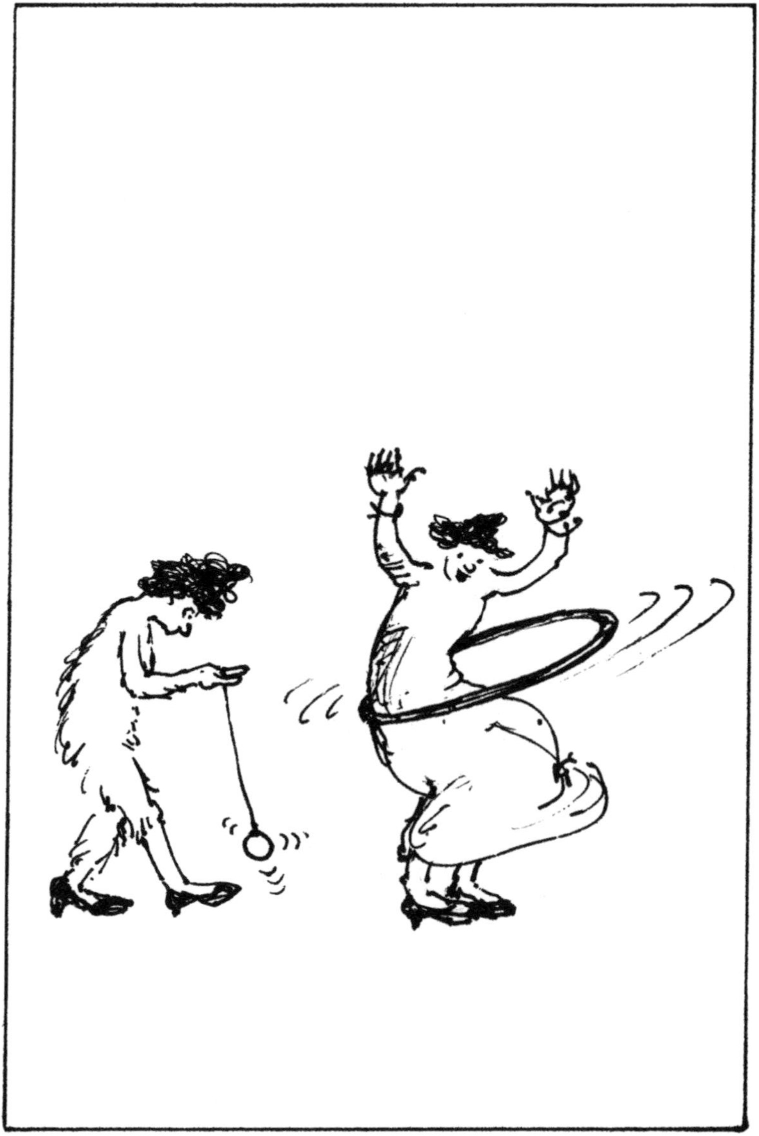

Darwin said if you made a list of eminent men next to a list of eminent women, it was obvious that men were better at everything.

Which was an odd conclusion for a genius to arrive at given the evidence available, and his five naturally selected ounces of extra objectivity. But he should know because he was a big monkey.

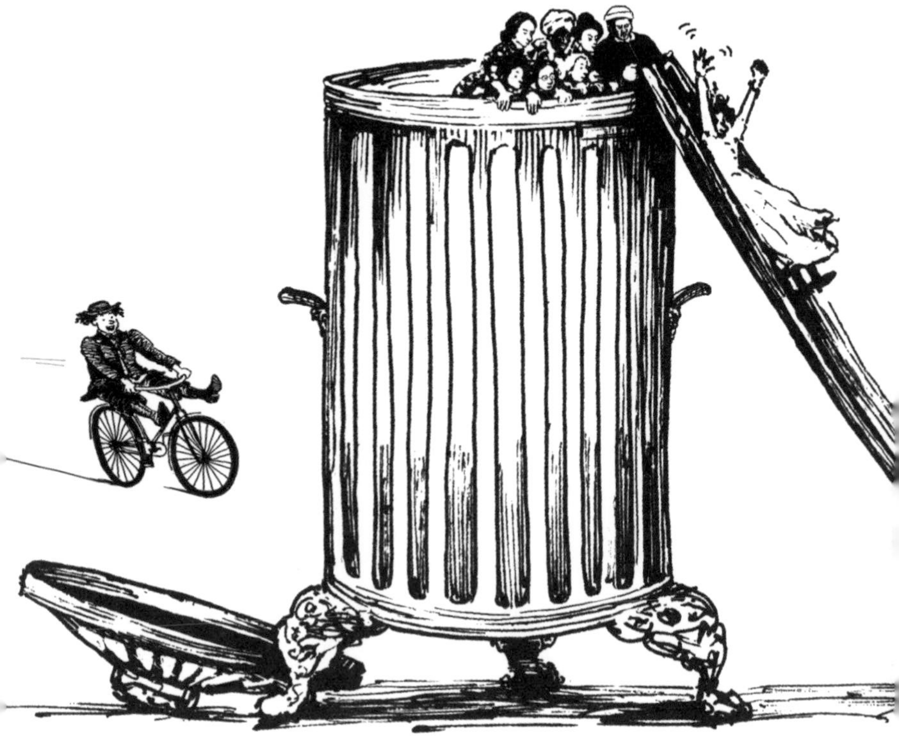

Andrews McMeel Publishing
a division of Andrews McMeel Universal
1130 Walnut Street, Kansas City, Missouri 64106

www.andrewsmcmeel.com

First printed in Great Britain by Square Peg, a part of the
Penguin Random House group of companies.

Jacky Fleming has asserted her right to be identified
as the author of this work in accordance with
the Copyright, Designs, and Patents Act 1988.

16 17 18 19 20 TEN 10 9 8 7 6 5 4 3 2 1

ISBN: 978-1-4494-7976-3

Library of Congress Control Number: 2016936004

Editor: Patty Rice
Art Director: Julie Barnes
Production Manager: Tamara Haus
Production Editor: Erika Kuster